Lifting

AS WE CLIMB

Mastering the Intimate Bible Study Dynamic

WILL SMITH

LIFTING AS WE CLIMB
Mastering the Intimate Bible Study Dynamic
by Will Smith

Copyright © 2014 William Smith

Published by: Beams of Heaven
Visit our website at www.beamsofheaven.com.

Library of Congress Cataloging-in-Publication Data: filed

ISBN-13: 978-0-9857429-0-4

Printed in the United States of America

Book Design by KarrieRoss.com
Book and Marketing Tips by Asha Tyson
Photos by Richard Brooks
Editing by Jason Sitzes

Dedication

THESE ARE DECEASED SOUL-WINNERS WHO
MADE THEIR MARK IN MINISTRY AND UPON
WHOSE SHOULDERS I STAND. EACH ONE HAS
HAD TREMENDOUS INFLUENCE IN MY LIFE
AND MINISTRY.

E. E. CLEVELAND
WILLIAM C. SCALES, SR.
ARNEDIA BROWN

Acknowlegements

I would like to express my gratitude to those who offered their financial support to this project. Without their sacrificial giving this project would not have been born. Nadean Johnson, Magalie Emile-Backer, and Jermaine and Bazi LeClerc, you were and are a blessing.

This book would not be possible without the support, guidance and encouragement of the following individuals. Their words of wisdom and holy example instilled in me a desire to write a book to help others as they have been there for me. They are William C. Scales Jr., Meade Van Putten, William Hall, Henry Wright, Melvin Janey, Gaylord Brown, Rudyard Lord, Amos Mackall, W. A. Thompson, Jasper Johnson, Robert Moses, Artemus Tucker, Kenneth Scott, Randy Howard, Rachelle Martin, Jenine Patterson, Fauzia Jones, and last but not least James Dykes, my Oakwood College English professor, who penned the words "You've been blessed!" on one of my writing assignments.

A project like this cannot be completed by just one person. I am forever thankful for those who laid the foundation for this book by their professional advice and service. Jason Sitzes, editing; Gwen-Marie Davis Hicks, copyrighting and business license; Karrie Ross, book cover design; Bazi LeClerc, marketing; Wanda Jenkins, Bible study lesson design; Angela Willis, website builder; Assaba Linda Akwei, developed power point slides for seminars; Taria Usher, Bible study lesson restructuring; Mary Opuni-Mensah, revising of Bible study lessons and marketing; David Barrow, revising and updating website.

Words cannot express my gratitude to my wife, Yvonne, for her loving support and encouragement. And the pats on my back for me to keep pressing on was appreciated when nights grew longer and longer because of writer's block. All the "Honey, are you working on your book? If not, you need to." All this gave me a burst of energy needed to complete this book after several years of blood, sweat, and tears. "Thank you Sweets!"

I dare not end this acknowledgement without thanking God; without Him not one word, not one letter, and not one thought could have been produced.

Foreword

Lt is indeed a privilege to share a few words concerning my friend, Pastor Will Smith. Early in his career, I invited him to serve as a Bible Instructor in several of our city-wide Real Truth Evangelistic Crusades. He was faithful, and his work, under the Holy Spirit's direction, was fruitful.

Since those days God has continued to bless him abundantly with unusual spiritual gifts in the areas of soul-winning, and training others to become effective soul winners. He is truly a role model in evangelism, because of his dedicated service to God, his love for his wife Yvonne and family, and his passion for reaching, teaching, and winning souls.

Surely this Soul-Winning Manual, under the blessings of God, will be a tremendous training tool for all who desire to lead men, women, and young people to Christ, baptism, church membership, and citizenship in the kingdom of heaven.

Elder William C. Scales, Jr.
Former Ministerial Association Director
North American Division
General Conference of Seventh-day Adventists

Table of Contents

Introduction

The Great Commission Jesus gave to His disciples was the salvation of men, women, boys, and girls (Matthew 28:19,20). Not solely a commission, but an opportunity to share with others the joy in salvation you have found. What is salvation? Salvation is deliverance from sin. Salvation is a gift given to free us from the entrapment and consequences of sin. And salvation is when we come to God and ask Him to forgive us of our sins and then accept Jesus into our heart as our personal Lord and Saviour thus restoring the relationship to God.

In seeking to ripen His disciples for the task of saving souls, Jesus said, "Follow Me, and I will make you fishers of men."[1] Almost two thousand years has passed since the Great Commission from Jesus, and we have not completed our task. Charles Spurgeon observed, "the heart is a fish that troubles all gospel fishermen to hold. It is slimy as an eel and it slippeth between your fingers."[2] Thank God that as a disciple of Jesus, you are willing to do your part by getting trained to be a soul-winner to catch slimy and slippery hearts. Amen!

I've thought about writing a soul-winning manual for several years, but procrastination had its way. But the drive to develop a guide to help others with this important calling that came directly from Jesus, to bring others to Him, overwhelmed me. I sat and I wrote. This book is for you. The person who has wanted to give a Bible study but never got started, the person who was ready to start but didn't know how, this book is for you, and for those who tried to bring a soul to Jesus, but the student was never baptized. The pastor who has a hard time baptizing one soul a year let alone reaching the conference or your church baptismal goal, this book is for you. The theology or religion major who wants to understand soul-winning and who wants to baptize one or more souls before entering the field, this book is for you. Is there a difference between soul-winning and witnessing? Is there a difference between making a friend and saying hello to a stranger? Of course there is. Witnessing is telling people about the life and sacrifice of Jesus. Soul-winning is bringing people to Jesus on a personal level. Witnessing is passive and soul-winning is active; it's tangible. Witnessing is passive in that most Christians share Christ on the job, at school, to the neighbor and to relatives and friends. Not only do they share Christ, but they live Christ-like lives. Amen! The person who witnesses will hope and pray those around will ask why they don't drink or why they eat canned hot dogs instead of pork hot dogs; it's passive. But the witnessing ends there. Anything more than passive conversation becomes active. Witnessing is very, very important.

Unsaved folks need to see a sermon and not just hear what Pastor Jones preached about over the weekend. Jesus need to be real in the lives of professed Christians. You will see more on this in chapter one. Witnessing is important. Witnessing is just not soul-winning.

Soul-winning is active in the sense that the soul-winner witnesses, but instead of hoping for questions and action, they take personal action. The soul-winner is aggressive in the sense of not forcing people to get baptized, but doing all they can to help the person begin active study of God's Word and make personal decisions within their lives based on the Bible study. In other words, the soul-winner not only talks about Christ, but once they spark interest in someone they ask if the person would like to study the Bible together. The soul-winner may say, "I've been noticing you watch me pull these hotdogs out of this can from time to time, let me tell you why I eat these instead of the pork hot dogs." Soul-winning is a mindset. It is a lifestyle of bringing understanding and salvation into the lives of those around us. Soul-winning is the fulfillment of the Great Commission!

I'm one of the pastors at Community Praise Center SDA Church in Alexandria, Virginia. In October of 2003, we (CPC) launched the Homeland Security Revival that lasted five weeks and five nights each week. Pastor Damein Johnson, one of my colleagues and former youth pastor at CPC, was the evangelist. Twelve Bible instructors, including myself, were used to meet with visitors and answer questions about the subjects preached, or to talk about what God had challenged inside them during the revival. I trained eight of the twelve Bible instructors on how to be an effective soul-winner for Jesus. God blessed us with over fifty baptisms at the end of the revival.

During the spring of 2004, a friend invited me to her church to train members in soul-winning. They were preparing for a revival called *Experience the Power.* Pastor Walter Pearson was the evangelist. This was a satellite revival that could be down-linked anywhere in the world. At my friend's church, we were only able to conduct a few training sessions before the revival began. Not enough training sessions for them to be effective Bible instructors and have a major impact for soul-winning during the revival.

Since CPC did not down-link the revival, I visited five churches that held the meeting to see how they were doing. The music was good. The giving of gifts to the visitors and the lesson study handouts was done in a timely manner. The registration process was well organized. The pastor or the elder did a fine job with the announcements. The ushers and greeters made you feel welcome. Deacons were nearby and alert to collect the offering and to handle whatever emergency that may arise. But as I watched the evening of great preaching and teaching end, visitors walked out with very few people available to talk with them. They left with questions and challenges unanswered. There were not enough Bible instructors to work with the visitors. Some churches had no Bible instructors. What an oversight!

To challenge visitors with the Word of God, knowing that God moved in their lives, and yet there were no Bible instructors readied to follow-up at that moment with these hungry souls.

I want this manual available to you every moment, at every opportunity, so that we can further fulfill the Great Commission of bringing people actively to Jesus and no longer being satisfied with the passivity of witnessing. And this manual is for you to learn to be an effective soul-winner.

LIFTING AS WE CLIMB

CHAPTER 1

The Call To Be A Soul-Winner

Begin now a daily prayer that God will provide a person to whom you can begin Bible studies with once you've completed this manual. Stop here, at this moment, and ask God for this person to enter your life within the week, or even today. Maybe this person is already in your life and you've suddenly become aware. Or you're coming to this manual with a burden already on your heart. Ask God right now to give you the conviction of beginning this Bible study once you've read to the end. Ask God to help you be an effective soul-winner.

Who would you be if someone did not feel the need to share Christ with you? I personally would be in a cold tomb without hope of eternal life in Christ. Alcohol and drugs would have killed me. And if you are honest with yourself something would have killed you or be killing you too. At the least, you'd be living without hope. You don't have to look far to see that people die hourly from alcohol, drugs and other self-destructive vices. Thank God you feel the need to reach these people and show them how to embrace the same hope you now have.

We sing, *Onward Christian Soldiers* and instead of enlisting we wait to be drafted into God's service. We sing, *Serve the Lord with Gladness* and complain when asked to do something. We sing, *I Love to Tell the Story* and never mention our story or Jesus' story all year. We sing, *Throw Out the Life Line* and are content to throw out a fishing line. Steve Vanderhorst, a friend, posed a question to me. He asked, "Adventists go on a lot of retreats but when are we going to charge?" I didn't have an answer for him at the time. I have an answer now and you have it in your hands. To prevent us from falling into the trap of simple passive activities, we need a clear and concise picture of what God would have us do in His plan to give the gospel to the world.

We must understand the 3 R's in the call to win souls.

We must *recognize*, become *responsible*, and not *resist*.

I. *Recognize* Your High Calling -I Peter 2:9

Do you believe that you are part of a chosen generation, a holy nation, and a royal priesthood? Christianity is an elect group. As part of this elect group you are chosen to be a blessing to those who don't know God. You are

a citizen of a holy nation. Our holy nation has blanketed
the earth with its holy presence. The king is Jesus Christ.
Are you a part of this royal priesthood? Not just any
priesthood, but a royal priesthood. You must *recognize* that
you are a spiritual priest for Jesus. As you meditate upon
this awesome calling you are to show the praises of Him
who called you out of darkness into His marvelous light.
The verse did not say, "tell" but "show" the praises of God.
Your holy life must emit light to those in the pit of
darkness, sin, and ignorance. *Recognize* that it is only you
who has been given the authority and challenge to give to
those in your life this message of hope. "There is an
eloquence far more powerful than the eloquence of words
in the quiet, consistent life of a pure, true Christian. What
a man is has more influence than what he says. The offi-
cers who were sent to Jesus came back with the report that
never man spoke as He spoke. But the reason for this was
that never a man lived as He lived. Had His life been other
than it was, He could not have spoken as He did. His
words bore with them a convincing power, because they
came from a heart pure and holy, full of love and sympathy, benevolence and truth. It is our own character and
experience that determine our influence upon others.
In order to convince others of the power of Christ's grace,
we must know its power in our own hearts and lives.
The gospel we present for the saving of souls must be the
gospel by which our own souls are saved."[3]

II. You are **Responsible** for Someone's Salvation-Ezekiel 3:17-19

God tells us to warn the wicked. That's a command; it's not optional. You are *responsible* to impact the lives of those around you; every soul with whom you come into contact will have your spiritual fingerprint. If you fail to warn the wicked and they die in their sins, God will hold you responsible for them being lost. It's one thing to be lost for your own sins, but to have someone else's sins piled on yours because of failure or neglect to witness, that's absurd.

"If sinners will be damned, at least let them leap to hell over our bodies. And if they will perish, let them perish with our arms around their knees, employing them to stay. If hell must be filled, at least let it be filled in the teeth of our exertions, and let not one go there unwarned."[4]

III. Don't **Resist** Getting Involved with God -Mark 16:15

Your world may consist of a few family members, neighbors, schoolmates or co-workers. Or you may have dominion over an entire company, or be the leader of a city. No matter the influence you have, you must not *resist* the call to involve God into their lives. Share the gospel with them. What happens if you don't? "Satan uses the listless, sleepy indolence of professed Christians to strengthen his forces and win souls to his side. By their failure to be diligent workers for the Master, by leaving duties undone and words unspoken, they have allowed Satan to gain control of souls who might have been won to Christ."[5]. In other words, by your *resistance* to witness for Jesus, you have allowed people to become emboldened in their sins. Thus Satan's forces are strengthened and instead of winning souls for Jesus, through your *resistance*, you've won souls for Satan. Either way, you're a soul-winner.

Once the call to witness is discovered in the soul-winner's soul, something else must be present. You must have a desire to save the lost. How is a desire to save the lost different from the 3 Rs? Your desire is what sets you into action. In other words, your desire makes you *recognize* your calling, become *responsible* for the souls around you, and no longer *resist* talking to those in your life, and the 3 R's become a reality not just a phrase you've memorized. A person can understand the 3 R's backwards and forwards and won't move until there is a desire to reach the lost. What is desire? Let me bypass Webster's Dictionary and give you the meaning from Napoleon Hill's, *Think and Grow Rich*. In the book he defines 'desire' as "the starting point of all achievement." A few examples of desire when it comes to soul-winning:

> "The Holy Spirit will move them by first moving you. If you can rest without them being saved, they will rest too. But if you cannot bear that they should be lost, you will soon find that they are uneasy too. I hope you will get into such a state that you will dream about a child or a hearer

perishing for lack of Christ, and start up at once and cry, 'O God, give me converts, or I die.' Then you will have converts."—Charles H. Spurgeon; excerpt is adapted from Steve Lawson's; *The Focus of Charles Spurgeon*

"The same intensity of desire to save sinners that marked the life of the Saviour marks the life of His true follower."—*Volume 7 of Testimonies to the Church*, p. 10

"In times past there were those who fastened their minds upon one soul after another, saying, 'Lord, help me to save this soul.' But now such instances are rare. How many act as if they realized the peril of sinners? How many take those whom they know to be in peril, presenting them to God in prayer, and supplicating Him to save them?"—*Gospel Workers*, p. 65

There are an unending number of fears that cause people to hold back when it comes to the call to witness. These fears are either innate (born in us) or developed over time. The tragedy of September 11, 2001, brought on a host of new fears. These fears include the fear of flying, the fear of being attacked again by a terrorist group from outside of American and within American and the fear of personal security. The fears in witnessing are not as frightening, but they certainly are real. In fact, the idea of walking up to someone and sharing the Gospel can result in the same physiological reactions. Sweating, shaking, irrational thoughts of outcome, and the inability to talk can occur when boarding a plane or talking to someone about Jesus. Imagine how different the two activities are and yet the physical symptoms of fears involved can be near exact. There are two major fears that stop people in their tracks when it comes to soul winning.

The first is the fear of rejection. Before I started the ministry, I was a part-time colporteur in my hometown of Baltimore, MD. A colporteur is a person who sells devotional literature, but I also sold health literature. My first door-to-door experience was unforgettable. While trembling, I knocked on the screen door as my mentor Robert Moses instructed me. Robert Moses was the Director of Literature Evangelists for the Allegheny East Conference of SDA. No one responded so I slowly moved to the next door or to the car, whichever was closer. Robert stopped me and said, "Knock harder!" I thought I knocked hard the first time; I certainly didn't want to disturb anyone. My trembling hands knocked louder and a man yelled, "Come in!" I froze for a moment trying to interpret what that meant. Robert nudged me and he followed, thank God. After a nervous presentation the guy bought the magazine. What were my fears? The first fear was that the person who answered the door would peek out of the door or a window and yell, "I don't want any, go home," (which I would have gladly done), and that the person would have rejected the material. Of course that would have felt like a personal rejection, not just a rejection of the magazine.

The second fear that people have when it comes to soul winning is the fear of not knowing, or not being armed with all the information. Not knowing how to explain your biblical position with supporting passages, or not knowing the answer to someone's questions. The Bible admonishes Christians to "be ready always to give an answer to every man that asketh you a reason of the hope that is in you with meekness and fear"[6] The Bible also says "study to show yourself approved unto God, a workman that needeth not to be ashamed, rightly dividing the word of truth"[7] If you study, will you not gain more knowledge thus saving you from shame? You won't be ashamed or embarrassed for not knowing how to deal with biblical issues.

When I was first baptized, I was viciously attacked by co-workers who believed differently from me. They attacked me because I did not believe what they believed. They attacked me by asking questions I wasn't yet armed to answer. Some of the questions I could answer, but others were difficult. I was put on the spot several times and was ashamed or embarrassed because I could not answer their questions with Bible verses. It's true that as a new Christian I should not have been expected to answer everything (even more seasoned Christians don't know everything). But I'm the one who professed to have the "truth." I did not like the feeling of embarrassment for not knowing.

The above two fears paralyze us from witnessing. If these fears did not exist, the gospel work would have been finished and we would now be in heaven. How do you overcome these fears?

Warm interest. These are people who have already expressed interest in spiritual things. These people are friends, relatives, and co-workers of church members. They are people who have perhaps attended, but never joined. These are folks who have attended prayer meetings or other church gatherings. Maybe they are the Easter and Christmas-only crowds. Perhaps they visit a few times a year. Also, be aware of folks who come to church week after week who are not members. They never responded to the altar call and they may never go to the pastor or someone and ask to join. It's all but possible they have fears greater than yours. These are the ones we are responsible for, remember the 3 R's? If we neglect them because our fear is greater than theirs, we have failed to trust God.

Not too long ago at the end of our first service (CPC has two church services on Sabbath morning), I was walking around speaking to saints in the balcony and saw a young lady whom I had seen before. I spoke to her and got her name then asked if she was a member. She was not. I told her who I was and asked if she wanted to become a member. She said yes, and we began Bible studies. Sometimes you just have to ask. There is warm interest all around us. Tackle warm interest before you take on cold interest. Please re-read last sentence.

Cold interest. This involves knocking on doors to gather interest for a Bible study, and it also includes "street ministry" (my colporteur experience was all cold interest). For instance, you stand near a mall and pass out tracts to whoever comes by and all you want or hope they do is take your tract and keep going. (Yes, this is passive witnessing. Nice job paying attention.) With cold interest you barely speak to the person. And you pray that they will say they want more information; you are often too afraid to ask. You will encourage them to call the phone number or respond to the email on the tract. And you pray that they don't ask you any tough questions. Especially questions like, "Why do you guys believe in the 2300 day prophecy?" Cold interest is important but I want you to get the feel, experience, and confidence in doing a Bible study and winning a soul or two before doing cold interest. I just don't want you to get discouraged from soul-winning by doing cold interest first. Cold interest has a way of stripping you of your dignity if you take rejections personally. There's a cruel, cruel world out there and folks don't care about you or your feelings when they reject what you are offering.

Another form of cold interest is doing surveys from door to door or at malls. The purpose of the survey is to gage the spiritual interest of people and possibly sign them up for a Bible study (see survey example at the end of the chapter). There are a few qualities you need to be an effective soul-winner:

DETERMINATION and ZEAL

> "Those in the service of God must show animation and determination in the work of winning souls."
> —6T 418

"It does not consist wholly in gentleness, patience, meekness, and kindness. These graces are essential; but there is need also of courage, force, energy, and perseverance. The path that Christ marks out is a narrow, self-denying path. To enter that path and press on through difficulties and discouragements requires men who are more than weaklings."—*Evangelism*, p. 479

GENUINENESS

"The unstudied, unconscious influence of a holy life is the most convincing sermon that can be given in favor of Christianity." —*Gospel Workers*, p. 59

"The influence of every man's thoughts and actions surrounds him like an invisible atmosphere, which is unconsciously breathed in by all who come in contact with him." —*5T*, p. 111

Have you ever meet someone and within minutes you knew something was not right? This is what is meant by "invisible atmosphere." They give off a vibe that they aren't for real; there is something phony in their demeanor. If your student feels you aren't genuine in the Bible study, you're toast. The worst part is that people may never tell you they questioned your sincerity; they never really opened themselves to God's Word because of how they felt about you. You complete the study and wonder why they don't get baptized. The reason, perhaps they felt you were a fake person the whole time. It could have been they felt you had a 'holier than thou' attitude. Or perhaps you reminded them of an overbearing parent or a snot-nosed child. It could be anything.

MENTAL CULTURE

> "If you take upon you the sacred responsibility of teaching others, you take upon you the duty of going to the bottom of every subject you seek to teach." —*Evangelism*, p. 479

When you possess these qualities and you find those with warm interest, and the Bible study is scheduled, what is the first thing you do when you meet the person? Build rapport.

COMMUNITY PRAISE CENTER SURVEY

How long have you lived in this neighborhood?

_____ Less than 1 year

_____ More than a year

What are the major problems in this area?

_____ Crime _____ Drugs _____ Youth Problems

_____ Other   Please Explain _____

_____

_____

Do you feel a sense of responsibility toward the problems of society?   _____ Yes _____ No

Do you feel that the solution to man's problems are

_____ Spiritual _____ Political

Do you believe in God? ___ Yes ___ No ___ Not Sure

Are you satisfied with your life as it is? ___ Yes ___ No

In what areas may we assist you or your family?

_____ Family Counseling

_____ Job Referral (Please give job preference)

_____

_____

_____

_____ Clothing or Food Assistance

_____ Place your name on our prayer list

_____ Free Online Bible Course

Name _____

Address _____

_____

_____

Telephone Number (   )_____

Email Address _____

Thank you very much!

CHAPTER 2

Building Rapport

Other than your student accepting Jesus as his/her personal Lord and Saviour, building rapport is the life-blood of your Bible study. Fail here, you fail. And remember that success is a mandate to us from God. It is our responsibility to be as effective as we can in soul-winning. That's why this manual was on my heart to give to you. We must show that we not only want to win souls to God, but we have a genuine care for those around us. We must, therefore, build rapport to be an effective soul-winner.

You can build rapport in the student's home or at a location outside of the student's home. If in their home, you can talk about how nice the home is (if it really is nice, don't lie). Ask: how long in the home, city, state; where are you from, why did you come here (if not covered earlier); married, any children, siblings; who is in the photos, if an aquarium, who likes fish, see a piano, who plays, etc. When at a location outside of the student's ask personal questions leaving out, of course, details of their personal home. I usually don't ask people where they work because some people are not proud of what they do for a living. We live in a society where certain jobs are praised and some jobs are frowned upon. If you ask about their job and you sense or see some uneasiness in the student, switch subjects. You spend time building rapport to get to know the person, and the person can get to know you and warm up to you. They don't know you nor do they know what to expect from you. You have to make them feel at ease. Listen intently as they talk to you; listening is key to building rapport. Become interested in what they say. You might even find common ground on things of great interest to you. If so, give all your enthusiasm of those subjects to the student. If you find you aren't connecting, share personal stories with them. Talk about your family, your interests. Tear down as many walls as possible.

Let's take a deeper look at building rapport.

"Every day brings fresh revelations of political strife, bribery, and fraud. Every day brings its heart-sickening record of violence and lawlessness, of indifference to human suffering, of brutal, fiendish destruction of human life. And while the world is filled with these evils, the gospel is too often presented in so indifferent a manner as to make but little impression upon the consciences or the lives of men. Everywhere there are hearts crying out for something, which they have not. They long for a power that will give them mastery over sin, a power that will deliver them from the bondage of evil, a power that will give health and life and peace. The world needs today what it needed nineteen hundred years ago—a revelation of Christ. Christ's method alone will give true success in reaching the people. The Saviour mingled with men as one who desired their good. He showed His sympathy for them, ministered to their needs, and won their confidence. Then He bade them, 'Follow Me.'" —*Ministry of Healing,* p. 143

If "Christ's method alone will give true success in reaching the people" then we need to study Christ's method.

CHRIST'S METHOD:

CHRIST MINGLED- JOHN 4:7-42; I CORINTHIANS 9:19-22

We need to meet the people where they are. They may not come to church right away. That's okay. And we can't be like the folks in Isaiah 65:5, "Come not near to me: for I am holier than thou." You lose if you feel that way and your influence is shot.

"The prince of teachers, He [Jesus] sought access to the people by the pathway of their most familiar association." —*Ministry of Healing,* p. 23

"He [Jesus] sought them in the public streets, in private houses, on the boats, in the synagogue, by the shores of the lake, and at the marriage feast. He met them at their daily vocations and manifested an interest in their secular affairs. He carried His instructions in the household bringing families in their own homes under the influence of His divine presence." —*Desire of Ages,* p. 151

CHRIST DESIRED THEIR GOOD
MATTHEW 9:35

With every person I give Bible studies to, I envision them getting baptized. That is why I am doing what I do, to baptize every person who sits across from me that expresses interest in the kingdom.

> "Jesus saw in every soul one to whom must be given the call to His kingdom. He reached the hearts of the people by going among them as one who desired their good." —*Desire of Ages,* p. 151

> "He [Jesus] taught in a way that made them feel the completeness of His identification with their interests." —*Ministry of Healing,* p. 24

CHRIST SHOWED SYMPATHY
JOHN 11:35

Sympathy is feelings for someone.

"None who listened to the Saviour could feel that they were neglected or forgotten. The humblest, the most sinful heard in His teaching a voice that spoke to them in sympathy and tenderness." —*Christ Object Lessons,* p. 21,22

"He [Jesus] spoke a word of sympathy here and a word there, as He saw men weary, yet compelled to bear heavy burdens. He shared their burdens, and repeated to them the lessons He had learned from nature of the love, the kindness, the goodness of God." —*Desire of Ages,* p. 90

CHRIST MINISTERED TO THEIR NEEDS
MATTHEW 9:36-38

Empathy is feelings with someone. Folks must know that you care for them in whatever they are going through, and your concern is not riddled with judgment but with empathy. Like a little ten year-old girl told her mother regarding a troubled friend down the street: "Mommy, I have her tears in my heart." That's empathy.

"There is need of coming close to the people by personal effort. The poor are to be relieved, the sick cared for, the sorrowing and the bereaved comforted, the ignorant instructed, the inexperienced counseled. We are to weep with those who weep, and rejoice with those who rejoice. Accompanied by the power of persuasion, the power of prayer, the power of the love of God, this work will not, cannot, be without fruit." —*Ministry of Healing,* pp. 143,144

"His followers are not to feel themselves detached from the perishing world around them. They are a part of the great web of humanity, and heaven looks upon them as brothers to sinners as well as to saints." —*Ministry of Healing,* p. 104

CHRIST WON THEIR CONFIDENCE
LUKE 8:26-39

It's hard to gain a person's trust not just in boyfriend/girlfriend relationships but life in general. It's a great thing if people trust you and have confidence in you.

"The fallen must be made to feel that it is not too late for them to be men. Christ honored man with His confidence and thus placed him on his honor. Even those who had fallen the lowest He treated with respect. Never did He utter one expression to show that His sensibilities were shocked or His refined tastes offended. Whatever the evil habits, the strong prejudices, or the overbearing passions of human beings, He met them with pitying tenderness."
—*Ministry of Healing*, p. 165

CHRIST BADE THEM, "FOLLOW ME"
MATTHEW 4:18-20

Jesus did not heal folks just for the sake of healing but he gave the person a call to the kingdom. That must be your goal; to see the person in the kingdom no matter what. But like Jesus, meet their physical needs first. You will see more on this in the chapter on the Bible study.

> "The Saviour made each work of healing an occasion for implanting divine principles in the mind and soul. This was the purpose of His work. He imparted earthly blessings that He might incline the hearts of men to receive the gospel of His grace." —*Ministry of Healing,* p. 20

> "Your success will not depend so much upon your knowledge and accomplishments, as upon your ability to find your way to the heart. By being social and coming close to the people, you may turn the current of their thoughts more readily than by the most able discourse." —*Gospel Workers*, p. 193

Once you build rapport with the person, give your testimony to confirm that you are who you say you are. In fact, your personal testimony is part of building rapport. The student has hopefully opened up to you, and you must open up to them. You've come out of a world that filled you with pain. Be brave to share your pain with them. Give your testimony before the Bible study begins or you can give it when you do the Bible study on Five Steps to Christ. It is the work of Christ "to heal the brokenhearted, to preach deliverance to the captives... to set at liberty them that are bruised" (Luke 4:18). It is our job to share this Good News of the gospel as an eyewitness to what Jesus has done in our lives. If you can't testify as to how God helped you overcome whatever the situation, what good are you in giving a Bible study? Folks need to see that Christianity is different from other religions.

Giving your testimony makes you credible during the Bible study. Give details about how and when your conversion took place; some details but not all details. You'll know what is enough to share to demonstrate the pain and hopelessness you felt before you gave your heart to Jesus. The student needs to know that conversion or the new life can really happen no matter what the circumstances. Especially emphasize things you did, or pain you felt, similar to the student. This will give them a tremendous boost knowing that if God took those burdens from you, He can take it from them. And as stated earlier, it helps the student to know that you're not just talking the talk, but you're walking the walk. When some professed Christians are doing some of the same things non-Christians are doing, a testimony can be a breath of fresh air and a major boost for Christianity.

I was at a gas station and got into a conversation with the cashier who was from Ethiopia. When I told her that I was a minister, she quickly said, "Do you drink, do you smoke?" I'm glad I was able to answer just as quickly, "No, I don't do either of those things." She scolded Christians in America for their hypocrisy. She said Ethiopian Christians were more serious about living for Christ then American Christians. In my experience, I sadly could not disagree with her. Hypocrisy is one thing that kept me from Christianity.

Of what should your testimony consist?

Consider these three things:

1. Your life before you accepted Christ (if raised a Christian, your life before you really met Jesus)

2. How you became a Christian (tell how it happened or how your prayers were answered)

3. Your life since becoming a Christian (tell of the change, the joy, and the blessings)

CHAPTER 3

How to Give the Bible Study

There is a fabulous study guide we've assembled that will help make you an effective soul-winner and your Bible study a success. Take a few minutes to order a set of *Lifting As We Climb* Bible Study *Lessons* for your student. Go to www.beamsofheaven.com to place an order. Make sure you and the student have the same Bible version when the lesson begins. For *Lifting As We Cliimb* study lessons, all of the questions are based on the King James Version. It's important to use the same Bible version to eliminate translation issues. If you use a different translation, you will have to explain almost every passage because of the different wording of the verses. The student can use the Bible of choice for personal Bible study, but the King James Version for the Bible study with you. A married couple interested in becoming soul-winners attended a Bible study with me. When I asked the wife of the married couple to read the Bible verse for one of the questions on lesson 1, she read from another version other than the

King James Version. The couple receiving the Bible study got confused by the different wording and I had to quickly explain it to avoid further confusion. It was my fault because although I told the students to use the King James Version, I forgot to tell the couple attending with me. All should use the King James Version for the lessons so all can be on the same page. No pun intended.

Bible study is not a sprint to the finish line. Take your time and make sure they understand the new things they are about to hear. Remember, we want a person to not only have a thorough understanding of God's love and sacrifice, but we want them armed with knowledge. Like I was uncertain as too many 'whys' of my conversion, we want to alleviate these fears in those giving their lives to Jesus. A person should not be baptized within 4-6 sessions of starting the Bible study. On the other hand, if a student is still taking Bible studies after 25 sessions, you may need to reexamine your approach. Pray about the Bible study and let God open your mind to new approaches.

Usually after about 15 sessions of the Bible study (of a 20 lesson Bible study series), the student should be leaning towards baptism and the Christian life. Please notice I am counting the number of sessions and the not the number of weeks or months. The reason for this is that cancellations will take place on the student's part and on your part. Rarely will you have a Bible study that goes exactly 20 weeks or 5 months which is one Bible lesson a week with a 20 lesson series. The devil will do all he can to disrupt and destroy the Bible study. Be patient and stay determined to continue no matter what and urge your student to keep pressing on. Some lessons may take more than one session to complete. If the student doesn't seem to be on the path of baptism after 25 sessions, consider the following:

Check to see if you are asking if each lesson was clear and if the lesson was understood by the student. This should be asked after every lesson.

Perhaps you covered the lesson on baptism and did not receive a commitment from the student, so you continued studying other subjects. With prayer, ask the student if they understand what it means to give their life to Christ. Ask them if they are ready for baptism.

You may not be conscious of the fact that the student may just love you giving them the Bible study and don't want it to end. In that case, let them know that after baptism you will be around and can still meet with them on occasion. Keep your promise.

Call or email me if none of the above works.

The only exceptions to not going through all 20 Bible lessons is a person who completed Bible studies before but never got baptized. With this person, you can review the lessons in one session to make sure they still believe and if they still believe, the person can get baptized. Also Adventists who were backsliders but now are seeking to recommit to Jesus and come back into the church or a person who was raised around Adventists but was never baptized. These individuals may not need to go through all 20 sessions but at the very least review everything with them to make sure they understand what God requires of them. The backslider may have questions about certain things so be sure to ask. It may take more than one session. But take this on a case by case basis. Some folk who were backsliders or who were raised around Adventists still may want to study the entire series and not want a review.

Show enthusiasm and a sense of urgency during the Bible study. Don't go in there all stiff. Let folks know that you are excited about being in Christ. Remember, you're finally doing exactly what Jesus asked. You're winning souls; you're fulfilling the Great Commission. You're standing in the world and reaching to a soul that wants to share your joy in Christ. Show genuine enthusiasm, especially when you hit topics such as conversion and the Second Coming of Christ. Show how excited you are that Jesus saved a wretch like you and how He pulled you out of sin and forgave you of all your foolishness and gave you another chance!

Let folks know how thrilled you are that Jesus is coming again to take you to heaven, for free, a place that you do not deserve. And that He's coming any day now so we all better get ready and stay ready! Don't take the Bible study lightly; you've been changed by the grace of God into a new creature in Christ. Your student, whom you have come to empathize with, who has possibly welcomed you into their home, needs to know that God is real and that Christianity is a happy religion and one that gives hope. We all have our personal issues and struggles, but there are too many sad and long faces from professed Christians. You should be thrilled that God brought you out of darkness into His marvelous light.

The Bible study is not a Sabbath School lesson. So take your time. As I said earlier, some lessons you may not complete during one session. I went to a Bible study with a friend whose coworker was interested in taking Bible studies. Her coworker was an older woman. As we went through each lesson, the older student didn't catch on as fast as my friend wanted her to. I had to tell my friend that the Bible study is not like Sabbath School, things are not covered as quickly, we have to slow our pace. Again, some lessons took more than one session to complete. This is true in general but really true with an older person who may take longer to process new light and in our case a Catholic woman who was not used to finding Bible verses. She was baptized.

In some instances you may have to pause in your lesson study to help the student understand a certain point. And by pausing I mean you don't move on to the next question until the student gets a clear understanding of their question and it may take another week or two before you can move on to the next question. A young lady seeking to become a soul-winner attended a Bible study with me. One night as we were going over the lesson on the subject of the Sabbath, the student, who also was a young lady, asked a question. Her question: "If today was the seventh day Sabbath, and we go back every seven days for 2,000 years, would we find Christ in church or would the days of the week be out of order?" She was asking if the weekly cycle over time lost its sequence. In other words, if today is Tuesday would it have been a Thursday a thousand years ago if you go back every seven days for a thousand years? I thought I was prepared to handle that question with supplement B that I give when I do the Sabbath Bible study. Supplement B is called, Has the Weekly Cycle Been Broken. We went through the supplement but the student still did not understand it. We delayed the Bible study on that question. Next week we came back and we thoroughly went through just the supplement again. But the student did not understand it and I really thought she would understand the supplement after the second time. During the next week I had to do more research hoping and praying to help the student understand. I found an answer she was able to understand. Thank God! Then, and only then, were we able to move on to the next question. Please note that I said we moved on to the next question and not the next lesson. We were stuck on one question for two weeks. What you just read may sound foreign to most of you but remember I'm talking about becoming an effective soul-winner for God. Like with guided missiles, you have to always hit the target and the target is the student's or the objector's question. By the way, the young lady was baptized.

If I have not said it yet, I'll say it now. This kind of attention to detail and patience with your student will not only enlighten the student and strengthen their foundation but it will help you to become not only a better and more effective soul-winner but it will help you to become a better and more responsible Bible student during your life as a Christian. That's why I discourage rushed Bible studies and baptizing the student with only a few lessons and moving on to the next student repeating the madness. This type of Bible teacher is robbing the student of the beauty of God's Word and the splendor of God's last day message for the world and robbing themselves of a more thorough understanding of the Bible and present truth. Like someone has said so eloquently, "It's not the destination, but the journey."

Be careful what you say. When using biblical examples the student may have never heard, highlight the story and make your point. Don't get too caught up into the story and forget the example you were seeking to give. It will only confuse the student. And beware of the Adventist lingo such as the Message, the Truth, the Three Angels' Messages, etc. Don't try to be theological. Beloved, the gospel is simple. "The lessons of Christ were illustrated so clearly that the most ignorant could readily comprehend them. Jesus did not use long and difficult words in His discourses; He used plain language, adapted to the minds of the common people. He went no farther into the subject He was expounding than they were able to follow Him."[8]

Enter the Bible study with confidence, certain of what you believe and take charge of the Bible study. You have what your student wants and needs so please be confident in your presentation. "Man up" (boys and girls) and teach the Bible knowing that God can turn the most hardened sinner into a saint. Remember, God turned Moses from a murderer to the meekest man that ever lived (Numbers 12:3).

A few more comments about the Bible study. Don't give out books during the Bible study. A few problems with giving out books during the Bible study. First, the student's focus is shifted from the Bible for the answer to the book you gave them and secondly, the student can show the book to their pastor or whomever and they can shoot it down saying we should study the Bible only and to disregard your books. That will put you in an embarrassing position during the Bible study. Let the Bible speak to the student, nothing else during the Bible study. Another problem with giving out books during the Bible study is that the student may become overwhelmed by books and end up not reading your books or doing the Bible study lesson and decide not to have the Bible study at this time. And because so many people think that we are a cult, let the Bible only speak to their hearts. Soon they will see that there is power in the Bible and the Bible only. The student will then respect our belief system and know for themselves that we are not a cult.

Two by two or can I go alone to the Bible study? Two by two is ideal but it may not always be possible. Just use a great deal of caution no matter how you do it. For instance, a guy wanted to receive Bible studies from a female church member. She was not experienced at giving Bible studies so she brought me along. The guy was no longer interested in receiving Bible studies; he just wanted to get with her and had little interest in the Word. It may have been quite a challenge for her if I was not there. So ladies, please don't go to a guy's home alone for a Bible study. And brothers please be very careful with going to lady's home alone. If you have to do it alone, give the Bible study at church which is a neutral place to avoid any kind of danger. At church while others are present either Wednesday night before Prayer Meeting, or whatever night you have Prayer Meeting or Sabbath afte noon. Again, stay prayed up so your mind will stay focused on the Bible study.

If you are giving a Bible study to a student whose spouse is the opposite sex from you be sure to build rapport with the spouse and be sure to invite him/her to the Bible study. Just invite a couple of times; don't keep doing it. Be sure to greet them every session if the Bible study is in the student's home. Beloved, I'm talking about being an effective soul winner. You can kill a Bible study by ignoring the spouse.

Should relatives give Bible studies to other relatives? If you can find someone outside the family to give the Bible study, let that person do it. Too often when family members give Bible studies to each other the Bible teacher will not be as firm on certain points as the person outside the family. If the family member has already accepted testing truths such as the Sabbath, the State of the Dead, and God's way of eating, the relative giving the Bible study may not be too quick to say, during the study on jewelry,

"Oh yeah, God's people should not wear necklaces or bracelets." That will be a challenging task for the relative giving the Bible study, especially if the relative receiving the Bible study is the wife, or the girlfriend or the mother. Not impossible for family members to give Bible studies to each other that leads to baptism but just be aware of these things.

How long should each session of the Bible study be? Each session should go no longer than an hour. Some lessons will take longer to complete then others. But once you're there for an hour, end the lesson and continue with it the next session. This timeframe includes building rapport, which you do mostly during your first session. After that it's just small talk before the Bible study begins like how was their week, how are the kids, etc. There will be times when the student's week or day was so burdened that they don't want the Bible study. You may be asking, "Why didn't they call me and cancel before I went to their home?" Sometimes they will and sometimes they won't. The times they won't call to cancel, they may still want you to pray for them or give them a word of encouragement. If you are a pastor, this is your time to minister. If you are not a pastor, and depending on the need of your student, have them read Psalm 121:1-8, Psalm 46:1, Psalm 27:1-5, Matthew 11:28-30; Philippians 4:19 or similar passages. Have your pastor call the student if these passages don't bring a sense of relief and comfort. That's why it's so important to stay prayed up. In addition to staying prayed up, if you don't build rapport and care for the whole person, you would not have sensed that your student is emotionally exhausted and have a different need tonight. Thank God on that night you did not miss a golden opportunity to show you're in this thing for real and that the person is not just someone to be given a Bible study to but a person whose needs you want to meet. Remember in the chapter on building rapport; Jesus taught us to meet the needs of the person first. What am I talking about? You got it right, being an effective soul winner.

Now, let's talk about how to start. The lesson begins. As the Bible instructor, you read all of the questions and Bible verses for lesson one. In other lessons you can let the student help you read, after you ask them if they wouldn't mind. If they hesitate, don't ask them again as they may not know how to read well or have some other issue. Let them know if they ever want to read or help read, they only have to speak up and you'll gladly allow them.

When you ask the questions on the lessons, give the student a chance to answer before you answer from the Bible verse. Sometimes students put the verse into their own words, and sometimes they write the verse verbatim on their paper. Either way is fine, just make sure they understand the verse whether they put it in their own words or verbatim. For example, question one in lesson one is: Who wrote the Bible? II Peter 1:21. If they answer, "God wrote the Bible," let them know that God did not physically write the Bible, but He inspired holy men to write it. However, remember that God physically wrote three things in the Bible. He wrote the Ten Commandments in Exodus 20, He wrote on the wall in Daniel 5, and He, Jesus, wrote on the ground when the woman was caught in adultery in John 8. If the student answers, "Man wrote the Bible," let them know man did not write his own ideas, but was inspired by the Holy Spirit to write.

If you have a partner with you, either one of you can ask all the questions and the other pray and comment when necessary. Do not interrupt your partner when he/she is talking. Please re-read the last sentence. Do not argue with your partner during the Bible study. A few years ago, partners I trained were giving a Bible study on the topic of the Millennium (1,000 years) in the home of a married couple and their 15 year old son. A question was asked by one of the students as to why God will allow the devil to live during the Millennium. One of the teachers said, "Because Satan wanted to be like God and have His power, and now God was giving Satan a chance to create." Another teacher said, "Where did you read that?" The two of them argued for a few minutes. The couple receiving the Bible study interrupted and said, "Let's end the Bible study tonight and continue next week." Thank God they invited them to come back. If something awkward like this should happen, call the student and apologize. Don't wait until the next session. If you disagree with something your partner says and you know they are dead wrong, don't be harsh and embarrass them during Bible study. You should handle this in one of two ways. At the moment the mistake is made, you can say to your partner "John, here's another way of looking at the answer to the question." Hopefully your partner catches it. Secondly, you can be silent during the Bible study and take it up with your partner outside when you leave and next week when you get back to the student's home, tell the student that a mistake was made the last session and you and your partner discussed it and make the correction in front of the student on that point.

To reduce the risk of these disagreements, partners should spend some time during the week preparing for the Bible study even if it's on the phone. Whether you have a partner or not, never give your opinions or thoughts about a Bible topic without giving the verses. With no Bible verse, silence is golden. Of course, because we're developing a life of soul-winning, my prayer is that you and/or your partner will conduct so many of these Bible studies once you've begun to be active in soul-winning, that the Bible study lessons will become second nature to you. The married couple and the 15 year old were baptized.

Finally, please note the one or two questions at the bottom of each lesson. There are two reasons for these questions. First, to make sure the student understood what you presented that night. Imagine going through all twenty lessons and you get to the end and your student didn't understand a thing you said. Why didn't they understand? They didn't understand because you never asked if the subject was clear or if they understood. You just assumed they understood. If the subject was not clear, please take the time to clear it up before moving on. This was mentioned earlier in this chapter. Secondly, by your student saying yes they understood, your student is getting into a "yes" frame of mind. And later when you make an appeal for baptism, saying "yes" may not be that difficult for your student because they were saying yes all along the way.

CHAPTER 4

The New Birth

You are halfway through this manual. Are you still praying daily that God will give you a person to whom you can get to know, and with whom you can share this Good News? One with whom you will begin these Bible studies after you've finished this manual? And are you still praying that God will help you to become an effective soul-winner?

Your goal is to bring your student to accept Christ as his or her personal Lord and Saviour and to enter into baptism. My goal is to see that you do it effectively. Why do I keep saying Lord and Saviour? The saving part has to do with Jesus delivering us from sin, and I use Lord because Jesus is the One who gives us direction, He is the One who tells us what to do. He is our Lord, and He is our Savior. That phrase alone in all of its understanding is the goal of the Christian; to embrace and to share.

Too many want deliverance but want to walk their own path once they come to Jesus. They accept this sacrifice, but do not accept His Lordship and willingly disobey Him. I will guide you through the lesson on conversion with the answers which are most important and central to everything the student will study. If the student is not converted within a reasonable amount of time after the study begins, you and they run the risk of them not understanding other truths that will be presented. That's why this lesson cannot be left to chance. The student's conversion makes it easier for them to comprehend and accept the more challenging truths. Paul says in I Corinthians 2:14, the natural man or the unconverted man is not able to grasp the things from the Holy Spirit (such as Bible truths) because spiritual things are spiritually discerned. Below is my lesson on conversion. Study it and be sure to understand it before you present it. This is true with all the lessons but very important with this lesson on conversion.

FIVE STEPS TO CHRIST

FAITH

What is faith? Hebrews 11:1

Faith is complete trust in God even when you have no evidence God is going to do what He says. Faith is belief that God will save me. Faith is belief that can save me. And faith is belief that God is now in the process of saving me. "Wait, God is in the process of saving me even if I have not accepted Christ as my Lord and Saviour?" Yes, He got you to the point of saying yes to the Bible study, so His saving process for you has begun.

How can I please God? Hebrews 11:6

By having faith in Him; if we have no faith, we cannot please God; John 20:26-29-Faith believes without seeing.

REPENTANCE

What is repentance? II Corinthians 7:9,10

Repentance means 'change'; it's a change of heart; remorse for sin; an awakening of our mind as to just how sinful we are. And repentance means a turning away from sin to God. The turning away may not take place right away but the person no longer wants to continue in sin; it may be an attitude change but real change is coming. On Sabbath, at the end of the sermon, the pastor makes an altar call for people to stand or to come forward to accept Christ as their Lord and Saviour or to receive Bible studies. When a person responds to the altar call, they are experiencing repentance. They want to change something in their lives. The changes may or may not occur that day. But most changes do take place during the time of the Bible study.

How is repentance accomplished? John 16:13

By the Holy Spirit. We cannot do it on our own. The Holy Spirit prompts any right impulse in us. Whether it is a desire to pray, to study the Bible, or to go to church, He is the one who prompts us to do it (see John 16:7,8).

Why do I need repentance? Psalm 51:5; 58:3; Jeremiah 17:9

Psalm 51:5 – Because we were born in sin. We have a slant or a bent towards evil that is incurable without

Jesus. That's why we need the Holy Spirit to lead us to repentance. In theology, the term "original sin" refers to the sinful nature Adam and Eve passed on to their children on down to our parents passing that nature on to us. That's why we have some of our fathers and mothers evil traits of character. Sorry, even if they are saints of God, they cannot pass on to you their righteous traits of character.

Psalm 58:3 – We come out liars, it is not a learned behavior.

Jeremiah 17:9 – Our condition is dreadful. The last clause, "who can know it?" Did you know you have no clue as to how evil you can be? Remember in the heat of anger you said or did something to someone and less than ten seconds later you wished you had not said or had not done it? You didn't realize just how evil you were. Thank God that He contains some of our evil so that we don't end up killing somebody and ten seconds later apologizing.

Is everyone guilty of sin and what is the result of sin? Romans 3:23; 6:23

Romans 3:23 – First part of the question-yes.

Romans 6:23 – Second part of the question-death.

CONFESSION

When will God forgive me of my sin? I John 1:9

God will forgive when we confess our sins. God not only forgives but He cleanses us of sin.

What are two conditions of having my sins forgiven? Psalm 51:3; Matthew 11:28-30

Psalm 51:3 – We must acknowledge the fact that we have sins and are a sinner.

Matthew 11:28-30 – We must be willing to give it to Jesus; the load of sin is too heavy for us to bear.

What happens if I don't confess my sins? Proverbs 28:13

God will not forgive us

What does it mean to have my sins forgiven by God? Romans 3:24,25

Instant acquittal; God no longer sees our past sins but He sees us as righteous at the moment He forgives us and He sees us spotless and not only that, He sees us as if we were always spotless.

CONVERSION

How does Jesus explain conversion? John 3:1-8

By being born again. A new spiritual birth has taken place.

How can I get saved? Ephesians 2:8,9; John 3:16

Ephesians 2:8,9 – By the grace of God; grace is an unmerited (unearned) favor from God. We don't deserve it nor will we ever deserve it. We must exercise faith to receive God's saving grace.

John 3:16- God sent Jesus to die on our behalf because He loved us.

What happens when I am born again? II Corinthians 5:17; I Peter 2:1,2

II Corinthians 5:17 – All things become new. Just as your newborn son, daughter, brother, sister, niece or nephew has new eyes, new ears, new feet, etc., so does a newborn Christian. The newborn Christian has new eyes by not looking at the same evil shows or evil movies; new ears by not listening to filthy music CDs; new feet by not walking into night clubs and unchristian parties. If a person professes to be born again and they are still doing the same things before the profession, they are not born again. (Bible instructor: Now is good time to give or repeat your testimony, especially the part where you became "new").

I Peter 2:1,2 – New born Christians must receive the milk (easy subjects) of the Word before eating the meat (more difficult subjects).

OBEDIENCE

What will I love to do after I am saved? John 14:15; I John 3:22; 5:3

John 14:15 – We will love to obey God. And that's why we keep His commandments because we love God. Spouses are faithful to the marriage vow because they love each other not because someone is making them do it. Obedience to God's Ten Commandments is our loving response to His love. The converted Christian does not feel that obeying the Ten Commandments are restrictive no more than a loving spouse feels obeying the marriage vow is restrictive.

I John 3:22; 5:3 – Because we love God, we want to please Him in everything and with all our hearts. And with the power of the Holy Spirit, it's not hard to do.

Did Jesus obey His Father's commandments? John 15:10

Yes, and Jesus is our example- I Peter 2:21

What is Jesus waiting for us to do? Revelation 3:20

Open the door of our hearts and let Him in. Jesus will not force His way into our hearts. In Holman Hunt's great painting of Christ standing and knocking on the door sends a beautiful message. The door represents the heart. But it's something unique about this door; there is no doorknob on the outside. Jesus can only enter our heart if we let Him in.

How should I live after Jesus has entered my heart? II Corinthians 5:15; Galatians 2:20

II Corinthians 5:15 – When I was a teenager my parents told me to guard my actions and to not bring reproach upon the Smith name. When we become Christians, we should not bring reproach upon Christ and His church. In other words, I should live differently from before. A definite change must take place. I should live for God and no longer for myself.

Galatians 2:20 – How can I know for sure if I've been born again? You'll know when the things you loved (drinking, drugs, premarital sex, etc.), you begin to hate and the things you hated (church, Christians, reading the Bible, etc.) you begin to love. And you'll know when God takes away the love of sin, the habit of sin, and the desire to sin. Medical doctors may be able to help us with the second, the habit. They tell folks that if you keep drinking you'll die from cirrhosis of the liver; then the habit disappears. But only God can help us with the other two. He can actually take away the love of sin and the desire to sin. How do I know, He did it for me. And "the life I now live in the flesh I live by the faith of the Son of God, who loved me, and gave Himself for me."

Do you understand the FIVE STEPS TO CHRIST?

- Have you already accepted Jesus as your personal Lord and Saviour?

- Do you desire to accept Jesus as your personal Lord and Saviour ? (If yes, you can lead them to accept Christ as their personal Lord and Saviour; see below.)

- Father, I know I am a sinner and I ask that You forgive me of all my sins (name some). I have no power to quit doing these things. Thank You for sending Jesus to die on the cross for me. I want Jesus to come into my heart as my personal Lord and Saviour. And please give me the Holy Spirit that I may be able to live for Thee. Father, thank You for forgiving me of my sins, in Jesus' name I pray, Amen.

CHAPTER 5

How to Handle Objections

To be an effective soul-winner, you need to know how to handle objections. A few things we need to clear up before we deal with objections:

Is your encounter with the person one and done? Will you see the person again? One Thanksgiving Day while in Baltimore, MD visiting my in-laws for the holiday, I had to go to a grocery store to purchase some Grillers because I forgot to purchase a Dinner Roast earlier that week. While in the checkout line a lady saw me with two little boxes of Grillers and asked me about it. I told her I was a Seventh-day Adventist minister and that we advocate a vegetarian diet. She went on to tell me that she was a Jehovah's Witness. I asked her about Jesus and how they viewed Him. She said that He was created and second in command in heaven. I asked her how she knew that. She was not prepared to answer me with verses. I wrote some Bible verses on a piece of paper where Jesus is acknowledged as God in their Bible, *The New World Translation* (the translators overlooked these verses when they were seeking to take out verses that pointed to Jesus' deity). I also wrote my name and phone number on a piece of paper if she later wanted me to discuss my questions (scold me for not having business cards). She never called.

Just in case you missed it let me tell you what just happened. The Jehovah's Witness had a question or maybe an objection as to why we advocate vegetarianism. Before she sought to put me on the defensive and have me explain our beliefs, I put her on the defensive and sought to make her explain her beliefs. Not that I couldn't explain our beliefs to her, I chose not to and besides, I wanted to go to the house and eat those Grillers with some gravy and work on those sweet potatoes or candied yams and the mac and cheese awaiting my return. I wanted to see what she was made of and not only did I want her to explain her beliefs, I wanted her to explain one of her most important beliefs. That is, the belief that Jesus was created.

This is what you can do to objectors sometimes, put them on the defensive. Stop pouring out your guts about our beliefs and the person doesn't accept it anyway. When they ask you about the Sabbath, instead of going to Genesis 2, Exodus 20, some New Testament verses, etc., say, "I have a question for you. Where does the Bible say that Sunday is sacred or that Sunday is our day of worship?" Step back and see what they say. If they don't know the answer, ask them if they need time to go home and study it. After you discuss and defuse Sunday sacredness, you can talk to them about the Sabbath. The Bible says in I Peter 3:15, "Be ready always to give an answer to every man that asketh you a reason of the hope that is within you." When it's a one and done situation, either leave some Bible verses with them or an email address or phone number where they can call you at a later time to discuss what you know God has given you as Truth.

Is it someone who doesn't want to meet with you? I was giving a Bible study to a married couple and the wife's co-worker had an objection with me teaching her about the literal, visible appearing of Christ at the Second Coming. The wife's co-worker believed and shared with her that Christ was coming in a secret rapture to take the Christians to heaven and the wicked will be left here on earth to have another chance to be saved during the Seven Year Tribulation. During that time the literal Jews will be restored as God's true people and go out to witness to the wicked and Jesus will come and get them at the end of the Seven Year Tribulation (see comment below on The Second Coming Objection Examined).

My student got confused. Since I didn't know where the Bible taught such a thing, I kindly asked my student to ask her co-worker to come over and explain his point from the Bible. The next week she told me that he was not able to come. I sensed he may be a little intimidated by coming into that atmosphere. So I told my student to tell the gentleman that we would gladly discuss these things at his home. Again he declined. Feeling that he may not be as sharp as he had hoped, I told my student to tell him to ask his pastor to join us for the discussion at his church. The co-worker declined the third time. Thinking her co-worker was not as serious as he appeared, she left him alone and accepted the literal, visible Bible view of Christ's Second Coming and she was later baptized with her husband. When the person that has the objection refuses to meet, do all you can to meet with them. But if they refuse, there is not much you can do.

Is it someone who you can meet with? Set up a time to meet with them and discuss the Scriptures with them. If it's a co-worker, you can meet with them during lunch. Here is a word of caution. If the objection is about the Sabbath, State of the Dead, Unclean Foods, etc., let the person know that there is a process for them to better understand if they start from the beginning and lead up to the point of objection. This is the ideal Bible study where you start from lesson one and go to lesson 20. If they don't want to start at lesson one but just want their objection answered, sit down with them and deal with the objection. But, be sure to get a decision from them to accept that particular truth into their life once you answer the objection from the Bible.

STATE OF THE DEAD OBJECTION EXAMINED

When you tell someone that their loved one does not go to heaven immediately after they die, they will quote to you this famous line, "To be absent from the body is to be present with the Lord." Did you know that this famous line is not in the Bible that's why I couldn't call it a famous Bible verse? Go to 2 Corinthians 5:8. It reads, "We are confident, I say, and willing rather to be absent from the body, and to be present with the Lord." Note, it does not say "to be absent from the body IS to be present with the Lord." It says to be absent from the body, AND to be present with the Lord. Read verses 1-8. You'll see Paul saying that he wants to get out of this earthly body and to be with the Lord in heaven.

SABBATH OBJECTIONS EXAMINED

Romans 14:5 – Based on these verses people feel that Paul showed proof that they can disregard the seventh day Sabbath. When verse 5 makes mention of "every day alike (implying the Sabbath can be disregarded)," does "every" always mean "every?" According to the following verses, it does not: **1.** Exodus 16:4; 22-26; **2.** 1 Peter 2:13; Acts 5:28,29 **3.** Genesis 25:5,6. No, "every" does not always mean "every."

Besides, Paul was not referring to the seventh day Sabbath. He honored that day and kept it holy. See Acts 13:42-44; 16:13; 18:4, 11; Romans 7:12. We must look at the verses within context (verses before and after subject verses). Paul was not telling the saints to disregard God's Sabbath upon choice. What was the issue? There was a dispute between the Jewish converts and the Gentile converts (Romans 14:1). The Jewish converts who were long devotees to the ritual of the ceremonial laws still felt they needed to obey those laws with its special days (Leviticus 23) to be saved. The Gentile converts did not have that problem.

The "first day of the week" is mentioned eight times in the New Testament. Do any of these verses call the "first day of the week" another name such as Lord's Day, Sabbath, etc. or is there any indication that the "first day of the week" became the new day of worship? Matthew 28:1; Mark 16:2,9; Luke 24:1; John 20:1, 19; Acts 20:7; 1 Corinthians 16:2 (the last two verses are explained below).

Acts 20:7 – Does breaking bread and holding a religious meeting on a certain day make that day holy? Not hardly, see Acts 2:46 (no title is given to this day). "Break bread" means to eat (Luke 24:30,35).

I Corinthians 16:2 – Look at vss. 1-5 contextually and Romans 15:25,26 (no title is given to this day)

Colossians 2:14-17 – **vs. 14** – Exodus 31:18; II Chronicles 35:12 (2 Kings 21:8);

vs. 16 – Leviticus 23 (vs. 38); **vs. 17** – Hebrews 10:1 (Genesis 2:1-3)

Objector: "Sunday is the seventh day of the week if you count from Monday." (Monday is not the first day of the week, Sunday is according to the calendar).

You: "Are you saying that Sunday is the seventh day of the week?" Then you ask, "What day do you celebrate Easter?"

Objector: "Sunday".

You: "You celebrate Easter because Jesus rose from the dead on that day, and the Bible calls it the first day of the week. But if you say Sunday is the seventh day of the week, you have to start celebrating Easter on Monday, the first day of the week according to what you said."

Conclusion: The point is they cannot have it both ways, either Sunday is the first day of the week and Saturday is the Sabbath, which it is. Or, Sunday is the seventh day of the week and they not only have to start celebrating Easter on Monday, the first day of week according to them but they have to start going to church on Monday, the day Jesus rose.

Objector: "Why do Adventists make such a big deal about the seventh day as the Sabbath? After all this time, the weekly cycle could be out of order and nobody knows exactly which day is the seventh day?"

You: "Well, if your point is true, that means Sunday is out of order too and you have to stop celebrating Easter on Sunday since nobody knows which day is which."

Conclusion: Review with the student supplement B of the Sabbath lesson. It is called Has the Weekly Cycle Been Broken?

FOOD OBJECTIONS EXAMINED

Romans 14:1-4

These verses set the context for the chapter – A dispute between Jewish Christians and Gentile Christians was the issue.

Gentiles, before conversion to Christianity, sacrificed and ate meats offered to idols. After their conversion, they no longer sacrificed meats to idols but they ate the meats that had been sacrificed to idols (these were cleans meats – Acts 14:13). The Jewish converts thought it was wrong to eat meats that had been sacrificed to idols (Acts 15:19,20, 25-29). This was the point of the dispute; animals *unclean* by *nature* were not the point of the argument but animals *unclean* in the *believer's view* of it. They felt those animals were unclean because they were sacrificed to idols. But, again, clean animals were sacrificed (Acts 14:13). The point of verse 21 is that we should not be a stumbling block to our brother or sister in the faith. Paul settles the food argument in I Corinthians 8:4-9.

Romans 14:14

vs. 14 – "nothing unclean of itself" – Those food offered to idols are not unclean of itself. Acts 14:13 tells us the animals offered to idols were oxen and oxen are clean animals. Again, the issue is not clean and unclean animals.

vs. 14 – "to him that esteemeth any thing unclean…"- The Jewish Christians felt it was unclean so they did not eat it but they were not to force their view on the "weak" Gentiles.

Matthew 15:11 (same story in Mark 7)

vs. 11 – "Not that which goeth into the mouth defiled a man; but that which cometh out of the mouth, this defileth a man."

Read CONTEXT (verses before and after the subject verse; read all 20 verses) for the ANSWER.

The issue is in verses 1 and 2. The issue was the disciples eating without washing their hands. The issue was not clean and unclean foods; unclean foods don't even show up within the verses. The Jews only ate clean foods and Jesus was talking to Jews. Jesus was attacking a tradition held by the church elders regarding eating with unwashed hands. The disciples broke the tradition of the elders not the Word of God (verse 2). Then Jesus talked about the Pharisees' evil hearts (verse 8, 17-20). In these verses, Jesus showed that it was far less important to eat with filthy hands then having a filthy heart. Filthy food may enter the body and may make a person a little sick physically but the filth that comes out from an evil heart defile a person spiritually.

Acts 10:13

vs. 13 – "And there came a voice to him, 'Rise, Peter; kill and eat.'"

Read CONTEXT for the ANSWER (first 28 verses)

Peter did not eat unclean foods at least up to this point (verses 13,14). That alone speaks to the above objection confirming Jesus did not put his blessing on unclean foods. Else Peter would have said, "I have never eaten anything that is common or unclean until Jesus approved it when He was here." Beloved, once again, the issue is not unclean foods. In verse 28 we see the issue. Peter, who had some prejudice challenges, calling people of other races common or unclean, discovered through the dream that "God hath showed me that I should not call any man common or unclean."

Divorce (Deuteronomy 24:1), like the unclean food laws, was a part of the ceremonial law or the Law of Moses. Was divorce nailed to the cross or ended at the cross? No, it did not according to Matthew 19:1-9 and Matthew 5:31, 32. These verses, along with the laws of the land today, show divorce is still in effect. And Acts 10:13, 14 and Isaiah 66:15-17 (see comment on VI) shows that unclean food laws are still in effect. A person can't have it both ways that divorce is still in effect and the unclean food laws are not in effect. The Bible teaches that both are still in effect.

I Timothy 4:1-5

vs. 1 – In the last days some church members will leave the church. They will leave because they were deceived by the false doctrines (teachings) of the devil.

vs. 2 – False teachers will emerge teaching falsehood in place of truth. Why? Because they are no longer sensitive to the influence and power of truth (**"their conscience was seared with a hot iron"**; similar to the effects of a branding iron where the branded spot is no longer sensitive to touch).

vs. 3 – The emphasis of these false teachers is centered in two areas:

- Forbidding to marry
- Abstaining from meats

Although the false teachers have a problem with marrying and meats, these are things **"which God hath created to be received with thanksgiving."** When did God put His blessings upon these two things? **Marriage**-Genesis 2:21-24; **Meats** – Leviticus 11 (God's blessings only on the clean meats). Note how eating the right things lead to holiness (Leviticus 11:44,45).

"believe and know the truth"- God's plans for man are best understood by those who have committed their lives to Him (John 7:17; 8:32; I Timothy 2 :4).

vs.4 – "every creature of God is good" – Yes, every creature is good for its intended purpose by God.

vs. 5 – **"for it is sanctified by the word"** As mentioned in verse 4, all creatures are good but only some are good for eating. Those "sanctified" by the word are the clean foods in Leviticus 11.

Isaiah 66:15-17 – Did the Penalty for Eating Unclean Foods End?

These verses contain a prophecy that points to the future; it goes beyond the Old Testament and beyond the New Testament down the Second Coming of Jesus.

vs. 17 – The *penalty* for eating "swine," "the mouse," and the "abomination (all other unclean foods)" is *destruction* and will be given when Jesus comes. Thus, the prohibition against such foods is *still binding upon all.* **NOTE:** Some say that because Isaiah is an Old Testament book this passage is limited to the Old Testament and have no meaning for us today. But this is not true because Isaiah 65:17-25 is also a prophecy that points to the future and it talks about the New Heaven and New Earth, which is also beyond our day. Content determines a passage's relevance not its location in the Bible. Else the Bible itself would be limited to Bible times only.

Colossians 2:16 – "Let no man therefore judge you in meat, or in drink…" Was Paul inferring that the "meat" ceremonies of Leviticus was "nailed to the cross" (vs. 14)? And that today we can eat whatever we chose? Two points must be considered:

The prohibition not to eat certain foods antedates (comes before) the ceremonial laws (see Genesis

7:2,3,8,9) . And the penalty for eating certain foods extends beyond the cross (see comment above on Isaiah 66:15-17).

The "meat" ceremonies in Leviticus were not meat (flesh food) but flour (see Leviticus 2:1,2,7). The word "meat" in the KJV meant food of all kinds. Note in Genesis 1:29 the word "meat" is used before there was death.

THE SECOND COMING OBJECTION EXAMINED

What is the meaning of the word Rapture?

The word rapture means to "take away" or to "snatch away."

Use of the word Rapture

The word rapture if left alone is a positive word. Jesus is going rapture His people when He comes the second time.

When the word "secret" precedes rapture it is a negative use because a whole theory is built upon it.

Through the years "secret" was dropped from rapture but the theory did not change.

What is the Rapture Theory?

It teaches that Jesus will come (unseen by all) and the Christians will disappear and fly off to heaven with Jesus and the wicked are left on earth. In the meantime, the literal Jews will be restored as God's true people. They, the Jews, will go out to witness to the wicked lost folks so they can be saved during what is called "The Seven Year Tribulation." At the end of this seven year period, Jesus will come back to save everybody who are now Christians and His people the Jews. And everyone will go to heaven and live happily ever after.

What Bible verses are used to support the Rapture?

Matthew 24:40,41

Luke 17:34-36

II Peter 3:10

Do the above verses make the Rapture a true Biblical teaching?

Matthew 24:40,41 – These verses do say that some-one will be saved and the other person is lost and left behind. However, these verses do not say that the person, who is left, is left alive. The Bible says in II Thessalonians 2:8, that the "wicked are destroyed by the brightness of His (Jesus) coming." In I Corinthians 15:51,52, the Bible says that when Jesus comes the righteous will be changed "in the twinkling of an eye." So to endure the dazzling brightness of Jesus' appearing, the righteous are changed instantly. And the fact that the wicked are unchanged; they are destroyed by Jesus' brightness.

Luke 17:34-36 – same as Matthew 24:40, 41 above.

II Peter 3:10- Note the verse says "the day of the Lord" will come as a thief in the night." It did not say Jesus' coming will be in secret; it says the DAY He comes will be a surprise.

The above verses do not support the rapture as a true biblical teaching.

WINE OBJECTIONS EXAMINED

THE EFFECTS OF ALCOHOL ON THE BODY

The degree and extent of mental impairment is related to the blood-alcohol level. Studies indicate that definite impairments begin at about 0.03 percent, which is achieved simply by drinking a 12-ounce can of beer or 5 ½ ounces of ordinary wine by an average 150-pound person. At 0.05 percent alcohol [about two drinks of 12 ounces of beer]...the peripheral (side) vision drops 18 degrees and depth perception 74 percent.— Rolla N. Harger, "The Response of the Body to Different Concentrations of Alcohol: Chemical Tests for Intoxication," 1964.

By one drink is meant the ingestion of the following amounts of the respective beverages which supply an equal percentage of alcohol to a person's body:

One Drink:

1 ½ ounces of whiskey

3 ½ ounces of fortified wine

5 ½ ounces of ordinary wine

12 ounces of beer

As stated earlier, one drink generally causes 0.03 percent alcohol in the blood of an average 150-pound person. Two drinks double the percentage. Kenny and Leaton report that at a 0.05 blood-alcohol level, "the 'newer' parts of the brain, those controlling judgment, have been affected." This becomes apparent, since a person "may become loud, boisterous, making passes; saying and doing things he might usually censure. These are the effects that mistakenly cause people to think of alcohol as a stimulant."—Jean Kinney and Gwen Leaton, *Loosening the Grip. A Handbook of Alcohol Information*, 1983.

Note how Proverbs 23:29-35 relates to the above statement:

29 Who hath woe? who hath sorrow? who hath contentions? who hath babbling? who hath wounds without cause? who hath redness of eyes?

30 They that tarry long at the wine; they that go to seek mixed wine.

31 Look not thou upon the wine when it is red, when it giveth his colour in the cup, when it moveth itself aright.

32 At the last it biteth like a serpent, and stingeth like an adder.

33 Thine eyes shall behold strange women, and thine heart shall utter perverse things.

34 Yea, thou shalt be as he that lieth down in the midst of the sea, or as he that lieth upon the top of a mast.

35 They have stricken me, shalt thou say, and I was not sick; they have beaten me, and I felt it not: when shall I awake? I will seek it yet again.

MEANINGS OF THE TERM "WINE"

The American Heritage College Dictionary, 3th Edition, 2000

Definitions for "wine"

a. A beverage made of the fermented juice of any of various kinds of grapes.

b. Something that intoxicates or exhilarates.

Merriam Webster's Collegiate Dictionary, 7th Edition, 1963

Definitions for "wine"

a. Fermented grape juice containing varying percentages of alcohol.

b. The fermented juice of a plant product used as a beverage.

c. Something that invigorates or intoxicates.

New Universal English Dictionary *of Words and Arts and Sciences,* 1759

Definitions for "wine"

a. Natural wine is such as it comes from the grape, without any mixture.

b. Adulterated wine is that wherein some drug is added to give it strength and briskness.

A General English Dictionary, 1708

Definition for "wine"

a. A liquid made of the juice of grapes or other fruits.

The above definitions of "wine" from older English dictionaries suggests that when the King James Version of the Bible was produced (1604-1611) its translators must have understood "wine" to refer to both fermented and unfermented wine not just fermented the way it is understood today. In other words, if you and me were placed in a time machine and taken back to 1611 and are studying John 2 in the newly published King James Version, we would have thought Jesus turned water into unfermented wine or grape juice (which He did) because that was the general meaning during that time. In view of this fact, the King James Version's translation of the Hebrew *"yayin"* (Old Testament) and Greek *"onios"* (New Testament) as "wine" was an acceptable translation at that time, since in those days the term could mean either fermented or unfermented wine. Today, when "wine" has assumed the sole meaning of fermented grape juice, modern translators of the Bible should indicate whether the verse is dealing with fermented or unfermented grape juice. By failing to provide this clarification, uninformed Bible readers are misled into believing that all references to "wine" in the Bible refer to fermented grape juice.

CHAPTER 6

Ellen G. White

Did you order your lessons yet? As you are daily praying to God for your student, He will deliver. You want to be ready the moment this person enters your life, if they haven't already. And under God, you will be an effective soul-winner. Visit the website www.beamsofheaven.com. In 1981, before I entered into the ministry, a church member's grandmother died and we were at her home praying for and trying to comfort the family. After the prayer, the grandson whipped out a newspaper he had tucked in his back pocket. The headline read, "Ellen White a Plagiarist?" The ironic thing was his deceased grandmother's name was "Sister White." The newspaper was from Washington, DC.

Not long after, my brother-in-law, Kenny, and I would take the young people out on Saturday nights for bowling, pizza, etc. One Saturday night while taking them home with one youth remaining, Kenny and I got into a conversation about Ellen White. We started shouting about some of the marvelous statements we read in her books. All of a sudden the youth in the backseat yelled out. "I hate Ellen White!" As it was, this response did not surprise me. This response is common among those not taught properly about Ellen White's role.

As you teach your Bible study lessons, you might find dealing with Ellen White can be very challenging. If for no other reason, you might find it challenging because it's not easy to introduce those just learning about Christ to a latter day prophet who appears outside of the Bible. You may feel it risky to talk about a prophet after the student has already accepted some truths such as the Sabbath, the State of the Dead, the unclean foods, etc. In my almost 30 years as a minister and having baptized over 1,000 souls, I have not had one person reject Ellen White as a prophet of God. Not one. Your approach to teaching about Ellen White will make all the difference in the lives of men, women, boys and girls. To see how I teach it, purchase the teacher's guide or the selected answers teacher's guide. The information below is for Adventists who are uncertain of her role or her calling. Everything below I hope helps you in not only your personal understanding, but gives you confidence to enter into these Bible studies. Remember, everything we do must be as informed believers and done with confidence.

HOW DOES ELLEN G. WHITE VIEW HER WRITINGS AND WAS HER DEGREE OF INSPIRATION LESS THAN BIBLE PROPHETS

"I have no claims to make, only that I am instructed that I am the Lord's messenger; that He called me in my youth to be His messenger, to receive His word, and to give a clear and decided message in the name of the Lord Jesus."

"Early in my youth I was asked several times, 'Are you a prophet?' I have responded, 'Iam the Lord's messenger.' I know that many have called me a prophet, but I have made no claim to this title. My Saviour declared me to be His messenger. 'Your work,' He instructed me, 'is to bear My word. Strange things will arise, and in your youth I set you apart to bear the message to the erring ones, to carry the word before unbelievers, and with pen and voice to reprove from the Word actions that are not right. Exhort from the Word. I will make My Word open to you. It shall not be a strange language. The messages that I give shall be heard from one who has never learned in the schools. My Spirit and My power shall be with you.'

"Why have I not claimed to be a prophet?—-Because in these days many who boldly claim that they are prophets are a reproach to the cause of Christ; and because my work includes much more than the word 'prophet' signifies."

DID ELLEN FEEL THAT HER WRITINGS WERE SUPERIOR TO THE TEN COMMANDMENTS AND HOW DID SHE VIEW THE BIBLE AND ITS WRITERS

"The Ten Commandments were spoken by God Himself, and were written by His own hand. They are of divine, not human composition. But the Bible, with its God-given truths expressed in the language of men, presents a union of the divine and human. Such a union existed in the nature of Christ, who was the Son of God and the Son of man. Thus it is true of the Bible, as it was of Christ, that "the Word was made flesh, and dwelt among us."[9]

"Written in different ages, by men who differed widely in rank and occupation, and in mental and spiritual endowments, the books of the Bible present a wide contrast in style, as well as a diversity in the nature of the subjects unfolded. Different forms of expression are employed by different writers; often the same truth is more strikingly presented by one than another. And as several writers present a subject under varied aspects and relations, there may appear, to the superficial, careless, or prejudiced reader, to be discrepancy or contradiction, where the thoughtful, reverent student, with clearer insight, discerns the underlying harmony.

"As presented through different individuals, the truth is brought out in its varied aspects. One writer is more strongly impressed with one phase of the subject; he grasps those points that harmonize with his experience or with his power of perception and appreciation; another seizes upon a different phase; and each, under the guidance of the Holy Spirit, presents what is most forcibly impressed upon his own mind—a different aspect of the truth in each, but a perfect harmony through all. And the truths thus revealed unite to form a perfect whole, adapted to meet the wants of men in all the circumstances and experiences of life.

"Yet the fact that God has revealed His will to men through His word, has not rendered needless the continued presence and guiding of the Holy Spirit. On the contrary, the Spirit was promised by our Saviour, to open the word to His servants, to illuminate and apply its teachings. And since it was the Spirit of God that inspired the Bible, it is impossible that the teaching of the Spirit should ever be contrary to that of the word."[10]

"If the Testimonies (all of Ellen White's writing should be included) speak not according to this word of God, reject them. But I do not ask you to take my words. Lay Sister White to one side. Do not quote my words again as long as you live until you obey the Bible. When you make the Bible your food, your meat, and your drink, when you make its principles the elements of your character, you will know better how to receive counsel from God."[11]

The following are excerpts from an interview conducted by the Review and Herald [official SDA Church Magazine] about Ellen G. White and her writings with Attorney Vincent L. Ramik, Senior Partner of Diller, Ramik, & Wight, LTD., specialists in patent, trademark, and copyright cases, Washington, DC 1981.

Review: What was your reaction after digesting all of this material?

Ramik: Well, that's an interesting question! I started out, I think, basically neutral on the literary charges. But, somehow, as I read on particular Adventist-authored defense of Mrs. White, it left me with the feeling that she was not, very well defended.

Review: What do you mean by that?

Ramik: Well, I came back thinking that Mrs. White was, if I may use the expression that has been used by others, a literary "borrower." And that she had borrowed a lot and that she borrowed with something less than candor and honesty! In other words—and this was before I had delved into her works themselves—I became actually biased against her in the sense that I thought she was what some people, such as her latest critic, Walter Rae, had alleged—guilty of plagiarism.

Review: Once you got into her writings themselves, was this negative impression reinforced or altered in any way?

Ramik: I gradually turned 180 degrees in the other direction. I found that the charges simply were not true.

But I had to get that from her writings; I did not get that from either the people who said she was a plagiarist, or the people who said she was not. I simply had to read her writings and then rid my mind of the bias I had already built into it—prejudice. And, in the end, she came out quite favorably. But it took more than three hundred hours of reading—including case law histories, of course.

Review: So it was reading her writings that changed your mind?

Ramik: It was reading her message in her writings that changed my mind. And I think there's a distinction— a very salient difference here.

Review: Would you describe the distinction that you see?

Ramik: I believe that the critics have missed the boat badly by focusing upon Mrs. White's writings, instead of focusing upon the messages in Mrs. White's writings.

Review: What did you find in her messages, Mr. Ramik? How did they affect you?

Ramik: Mrs. White moved me! In all candor, she moved me. I am a Roman Catholic; but, Catholic, Protestant, whatever—she moved me. And I think her writings should move anyone, unless he is permanently biased and is unswayable.

Review: Would you explain what you mean by this?

Ramik: Well, a person can walk this earth doing good deeds and saying to himself (and maybe to others): "I'm a nice person." And after a time you really come to believe that you are. But when was the last time that you really looked inside yourself and found out what you were really like? Now, there are a lot of things that Mrs. White has put down on paper that will, if read seriously, perhaps cause a person to look inwardly, honestly. And if you do, the true self comes out. I think I know a little more today about the real Vincent Ramik than I did before I started reading the message of Ellen White, not simply her writings.

Review: Attorney Ramik, how would you sum up the legal case against Ellen White as far as the charges of plagiarism, piracy, and copyright infringement are concerned?

Ramik: If I had to be involved in such a legal case, I would much rather appear as defense counsel than for the prosecution. There simply is no case!

CHAPTER 7

Getting Decisions for Baptism

When I started the ministry, I found out that some of the people on the Allegheny East Conference Executive Committee wanted to know if I knew how to bring a soul across the line. What that means is they wanted to know if I knew how to bring a soul to a decision for baptism. This is crucial for a soul-winner. If you are uncertain how to win souls, you must begin putting this manual into practice so that you learn to be an effective soul-winner. Remember, the souls of those around us have our spiritual fingerprint on them. We are responsible as a mandate from God to not just witness to them, but to be active in winning souls. The following information is very important to your success as a soul-winner. Be sure to study it over and over again until it becomes second nature.

METHODS IN GETTING DECISIONS FOR BAPTISM

The following information is taken from; *SOUL-WINNING MADE EASIER*, by Kembleton S. Wiggins, former evangelist, Inter-American Division of Seventh-day Adventist.

FFF TECHNIQUE

"This technique is replying to an objection with FFF. "Mr. Jones, I understand how you FEEL (first F). Many others (include yourself if it applies) in your situation have FELT (second F) exactly the same way. But, Mr. Jones, they have FOUND (third F) that Jesus gave them strength to get baptized and they never looked back." You may can use your own story for this section.

OJECTIONS VERSES EXCUSES

"Many soul-winners cannot distinguish between real objections and mere excuses. We should understand that the techniques for handling them are quite different. The objection is an honest block to a strong decision. The soul-winner cannot secure a decision until the block is removed. The prospect is convinced that the objection is valid, and you should take it seriously. Objections may be based on 1. Failure of the person to see the need for the decision; 2. A dislike of certain characteristics of the Seventh-day Adventist Church he is being asked to join; 3. Social, economic, or family problems he sees to be part of the consequences of the action you desire; or 4. Insufficient motivation.

"The three dominant factors in decision making are 1. Attitude toward the action 2. The expectation of a significant other, 3. The motivation to comply with the expectation. Hence all significant objections must be in one or more of those areas. Your job is to determine in which area the objection lies and answer it in a way that leaves that particular variable weighted toward a favorable decision.

"An excuse, on the other hand, is an attempt to avoid making a decision. Do not be annoyed by excuses, for they are evidence that the person is in the valley of decision. The important things to remember are that you should not argue with a person offering the excuse. Don't even try to answer excuses.

"Experience is the best teacher of differentiating between an objection and an excuse. However, the person's attitude and timing are good guidelines."

The following may seem simple but it is too often overlooked or neglected when it comes to getting folks baptized. When the person completes the Bible study series, ask the person how he or she feels about being baptized into the Seventh-day Adventist church or what will keep them from being baptized into the Seventh-day Adventist church? Then listen to the answer. If the person says yes, move forward. If the person says no, find out why and move forward when you can. As stated earlier, make sure you have an objection and not an excuse. Re-read that section if you have to.

Now What?

You've prayed for the soul that God wants to provide so you can become an effective soul-winner, and not just someone who witnesses. You've armed yourself with techniques and you've studied the Bible study you'll soon use. You've learned the 3 R's, and you've learned how to approach your first Bible study. It's very possible that by the time you finish this last page that someone will walk up to you with pain in their eyes; then you must not resist. You've been praying for God to lead you to this person since you purchased this manual. By now, you should have the teacher's guide lessons and at least one set for your Bible student. Schedule a time to meet with the person and be sure to tell your pastor that you are giving a Bible study. If you do not have a person at this point to do Bible studies with, call your pastor and ask about the list of names of people who responded to the altar calls (appeals) at church over the last six months. Only deal with the ones who have warm interest, those who checked baptism or an interest in Bible studies. Ask about the list of people who attended a recent evangelistic series, but did not get baptized. Ask about the list of non-Adventists who attend Prayer Meeting on a regular basis. Ask about the list of names the pastor received from Voice of Prophecy, Amazing Facts, It is Written, etc.

Schedule a time to meet with your pastor in his or her office. Review each name and get your pastor to determine if this is an A, B, C, or D interest. A and B interests are warm interests and C and D are the cold interests. Your focus will be on the A and B interests. When you get the lists, you begin calling these people to see if they are still interested in Bible studies as they checked on the appeal card, or as they expressed interest through some other means. As you call, identify yourself from the church and let them know how you received their name. Don't forget, begin building the rapport upon first contact. Your essential thrust is to be genuine from the first meeting. You will no doubt gather at least one Bible study from this large group of folks. The reason you will gather at least one Bible study from this group is because God is going to honor your daily prayers for a person to give a Bible study to.

In a few months your first Bible study student will be preparing for baptism. Please let me know the date of the baptism because I would love to attend if I can. What a celebration we'll have when your student comes up out of the water!

Beloved, I want to enter into a long term relationship with you; I want to be your supplier for soul-winning materials for as long as you use and need them. And I will do whatever it takes within reason to establish a relationship with you and make it work.

In closing, do you know two or three people in a similar situation like you who might benefit from this soul-winning information? Please tell them how this manual has helped you and please point them to my website at www.BeamsofHeaven.com. Thank you for purchasing this soul-winning manual. May God richly bless you as you begin this life changing ministry!

Endnotes

[1] Matthew 4:19

[2] Charles Spurgeon; *"The Power of the Holy Ghost"*; Spurgeon Sermons, Volume 1

[3] *Ministry of Healing*, p. 469.

[4] Charles Spurgeon, *Spurgeon at His Best*; compiled by Tom Carter, 1988

[5] *Christian Service*, p. 37

[6] I Peter 3:15

[7] II Timothy 2:15

[8] *Gospel Workers*, p. 169

[9] John 1:14

[10] *The Great Controversy*, pp. v-vii.

[11] *Selected Messages Book Three,* pp. 32,33

ABOUT THE AUTHOR

PASTOR SMITH received his ministerial and theological training at Oakwood College (now Oakwood University) in Huntsville, AL. He has been a minister for amost 30 years. He started the ministry in 1986 when Elder Meade Van Putten, president of the Allegheny East Conference of Seventh-day Adventists, gave him a call to that field in the city of Wilmington, DE. Elder William C. Scales Jr. (retired Ministerial Director for the North American Division) was very instrumental in helping him get into the ministry. Pastor Smith worked with Elder Scales as a Bible instructor in several city-wide evangelistic meetings. Over two hundred precious souls were baptized in each of the first two evangelistic meetings; over one hundred were baptized in the third. The first city-wide evangelistic meeting he worked in with Elder Scales, in Baltimore, MD, was the spark that lit Pastor Smith's fire. From there he has worked in 24 evangelistic meetings and was the head Bible instructor in 12 of those meetings. Pastor Smith has held four Revelation Seminars and 50 precious souls were baptized in total.

Currently Pastor Smith is on the pastoral staff at the Community Praise Center (CPC) SDA Church located in Alexandria, VA. He is a specialist and expert at doing Bible studies and preparing people for baptism. God blessed Pastor Smith to baptize more than 1,000 souls during the almost 30 years of his ministry. He is also skilled at teaching others how to become soul-winners (see Testimonials on website: www.BeamsofHeaven.com).

Pastor Smith was born and raised in Baltimore, MD. Growing up in the Catholic Church, at the age of 10 he declined his mother's appeal for him to be baptized. As a result, he began a life that quickly spiraled downward. During his teen years he would drink alcohol three times a day and doubled on weekends. Marijuana was also a part of his ritual. Early on he had control of his alcohol consumption but later it controlled him. There was no relief in sight. Then his mother died four months before his high school graduation. This made him take a serious look at his life.

A couple of years later his future brothers and sisters in-law encouraged Pastor Smith to try Jesus. They lived the life they professed. He didn't think Jesus could help his case. Who could help him with all the drinking and marijuana and partying? When he accepted Jesus as his personal Lord and Saviour, God took away the alcohol, marijuana and the negative lifestyle the same day. Thank God! His brothers and sisters-in-law are, Melvin and Mille Janey (Melvin is currently a pastor in the Allegheny East Conference of Seventh-day Adventists) and Kenneth and Marion Scott. Melvin gave him Bible studies. The Seventh-day Adventist church's high standard and the consistent Christian life of his future in-laws is what appealed to Pastor Smith. He got baptized into the Edmondson Heights Seventh-day Adventist Church in Baltimore, MD and he never looked back. He did not join the Catholic Church which disappointed his father. As a result, his father did not attend his baptism or his wedding.

Pastor Smith had to fight to get the Sabbath off and after a number of weeks, God came through and he kept his job but no longer had to work on Sabbath. Also thank God for Pastor Rudyard Lord, his pastor at the time, for standing by his side in helping him get the Sabbath off. During the time of negotiations, he did not work on the Sabbath.

Pastor Smith is married to Yvonne, and lives in Fort Washington, MD. They have two grown sons Will Jr. and Aaron. Will lives in Baltimore, MD and Aaron lives in Los Angeles, CA.

Visit Pastor Smith's website at:

www.BeamsofHeaven.com

17512901R00064

Made in the USA
Middletown, DE
28 January 2015